TROUBLED

SOCIETY

TOXIC
WASTE

George H. Jenkins

The Rourke Corporation, Inc.
Vero Beach, Florida 32964

Hundredfold *2/21/97* *16.65*

The Rourke Corporation, Inc.
P.O. Box 3328, Vero Beach, FL 32964

Jenkins, George H., 1950-
    Toxic waste / by George H. Jenkins.
        p. cm. — (Troubled society)
    Includes index.
    Summary: Examines the origins and dangers of toxic and hazardous wastes and what can be done about them.
    ISBN 0-86593-111-9
    1. Hazardous wastes—Juvenile literature. [1. Hazardous wastes. 2. Pollution.] I. Title. II. Series.
TD1030.5.J46 1991
363.72'87—dc20   91-12172
                                                                                     CIP
                                                                                     AC

Series Editor: Gregory Lee
Editors: Elizabeth Sirimarco, Marguerite Aronowitz
Book design and production: The Creative Spark,
    Capistrano Beach, CA
Cover photograph: Jack Swenson/Tom Stack & Associates

Contents

ONE

WHAT IS TOXIC WASTE?

Fortunately, the accident didn't cause a death. After the initial panic of concern, you and your friends pause to watch as police and fire officials work to pry a trapped driver from his now-mangled car. The car had careened out of control and sheared a power pole into two pieces. The police and firefighters are keeping onlookers from the wreck and have roped off a large cylinder at the end of the power pole. The cylinder is broken and spilling a foul smelling liquid in the rain gutter. Someone asks a police officer why the power pole is being protected. He answers, "It's *toxic*."

Toxic? Your mind is full of questions. What's toxic? Why is everyone so frightened? The police are acting like the foul goo is poison. Another fire vehicle arrives with sirens screaming and lights flashing. The police make way for the new truck. It has large letters on the side that say HAZ MAT. Smaller letters on the back of the truck say DANGER: HAZARDOUS MATERI-ALS. The cylinder has new meaning to you. Whatever that stuff is, the authorities believe it's dangerous. A friend points out the hundreds of times you and others have walked under that pole, unaware that you were so close to a harmful substance.

You continue to look on with fascination as the firefighters begin to dress in protective suits that cover their entire bodies. Breathing equipment is added. Like aliens from space they waddle toward the mysterious cylinder.

Soon the mess is cleaned up, the cylinder removed, and the car towed away. The driver is shaken but not badly hurt. This event, and others like it,

Firefighters have special equipment to protect them from hazardous spills that require emergency cleanup.

occur hundreds of times each year, unnoticed by most of the general public. The men and women who risk their health and sometimes their lives handling hazardous materials can be found in every community in the United States. They are an unseen army of professionals who deal with only a small part of what is becoming a very real problem: What to do with America's toxic waste.

A Special Kind Of Pollution

Toxic waste is a growing part of a much larger problem—pollution. When seen from space our world looks like a beautiful blue, white, and brown marble. Even from space, however, we can see signs of the damage caused by pollution. There is the brown-gray smudge of smog over most of the world's cities; the shiny greenish-blue of pesticides that pour out of the Mississippi Delta into the Gulf of Mexico; the black clouds caused by oil fires in Kuwait.

Closer to home, you are probably aware of smog—if not in your town, at least in a city you have visited. You know about litter along the highways and on the grounds of your own school. All this is part of the greater problem of pollution. This garbage, or waste, is generated by the people and machines that make up our industrialized world.

Each year the United States alone generates about 220 million tons of garbage. This figure represents only the solid or liquid trash that must be managed. It does not include the billions of tons of *particulates* (particles) that are ejected into the atmosphere by factory smokestacks and automobile tailpipes. In time, even the tons of pollution that go into the air return to the earth as *acid rain*. Acid rain damages thousands of acres of forest, orchards and crops each year. It also pollutes the water, killing fish and other creatures who live in rivers, streams and lakes. Many fishing and recreational sites have been ruined by acid rain. And acid rain doesn't respect international borders—particulates from American industries fall on Canadian land, and vice versa. Waste from the Soviet Union causes damage in Sweden and even Great Britain.

The pollution problem is both large and complex. A small but important part of this problem is toxic waste. Anything toxic is poison, and that means it is harmful to life. When the HAZ MAT truck hauls away a load of harmful chemicals, the problem does not just go away. If poorly stored and disposed of, that very load of chemicals may one day end up in your drinking water.

How do we protect people from accidental exposure to toxic wastes? To answer this question, we must understand how *toxins* are created, what they are, how to use and transport them safely, and how to dispose of them safely.

The high cost of storing and disposing of large amounts of toxic waste generated each year is forcing our society to find new ways of manufacturing. Changes in technology can minimize the creation of toxins.

What Is Hazardous?

Many chemicals manufactured today were once considered to be harmless, but with modern

Toxic waste can take many forms, including the countless containers that originally held toxic substances such as solvents, pesticides, and motor oil. Just throwing away empty containers like these does not eliminate the problem of toxic waste.

research they have been found to be toxic. So it is important that we continue to research how the chemicals we create impact our environment. The Environmental Protection Agency (EPA) has special definitions of what hazardous wastes are. Waste is considered to be hazardous if it exhibits one or more of the following characteristics:

- *Ignitability.* Ignitable wastes can create fires under certain conditions. Examples include liquids like cleaning solvents and friction-sensitive substances that can act like matches.
- *Corrosivity.* Corrosive wastes include those that are acidic and those that are capable of corroding metal containers.
- *Reactivity.* Reactive wastes are unstable under everyday conditions. They can create explosions and/or toxic fumes, gases, and vapors when mixed with water.
- *Toxicity.* Toxic wastes are harmful or fatal when swallowed or *ingested*, or absorbed. When toxic wastes are disposed of on land, contaminated liquid may drain or *leach* from the waste and pollute ground water. Toxicity is identified through a laboratory procedure called the *extraction procedure toxicity test.*

According to EPA estimates, about 250 million tons of the six billion tons of industrial, agricultural, commercial and domestic wastes we generate annually are classified as "hazardous."

TWO

WHERE DOES IT COME FROM?

Most of us think the solution to waste disposal is the nearest trash can. Garbage discarded from American households is, for the most part, the most visible source of trash in our lives.

Of the countless tons of garbage disposed of each year, a small but significant percentage can be classified as toxic. In the United States alone, over 292 million tons of toxic wastes are generated each year—or over one ton for each U.S. citizen! Most of these toxic materials are chemicals created for use in manufacturing, assembling, packaging, and trans-porting almost everything we use each day. These materials include:

- oil and oil byproducts such as plastic;
- pesticides, used in agriculture and gardens;
- acids, used in manufacturing for etching, leaching, etc.;
- minerals such as lead, chrome, and asbestos, used in manufacturing;
- toxic elements that appear in nature, such as selenium and radon.

A common characteristic of all these materials is that in certain combinations and quantities, they are all hazardous to life. These hazards affect each of us in two basic ways: direct contact and indirect contact. The chemicals contained in that power pole cylinder may cause skin burn or cancer if direct con-tact occurs. That is why special suits are used to pro-tect those who must handle the material in such an accident. The second hazard is not so visible. Any of the material from the cylinder that escaped into the

The United States has literally thousands of hazardous waste sites that are unsafe for humans to live around. This sign warns motorists near St. Louis to take precautions.

rain gutter has a good chance of contaminating the local ground water. Eventually it can end up in our water supply.

Ground Water Pollutants

Since direct contact with most toxic wastes rarely happens, however, let's examine the effect, source, and solutions of toxins in ground water. There are almost as many sources of toxic pollution as there are people in the United States. The following represents just a few of the ways that toxins can end up in your ground water:

▪ *Injection wells.* Injection wells are the most common

method used to dispose of toxic wastes. These wells are drilled far underground, below the earth's normal ground water levels. Toxic wastes are pumped down into these wells for permanent storage. It is hoped that by using this method, the materials will be buried deep enough and not cause harm to the environment. Approximately 10 billion gallons of wastes, or about 58 percent of all liquid toxic waste disposed of each year, are disposed of this way.

There are about 250 injection wells in the United States. Most of these wells (about 66 percent) are in Texas and Louisiana. The rest are in Ohio, Michigan, Indiana, Illinois, and Oklahoma.

The problem of waste disposal using this method is that even today, what actually happens to these injected wastes is not clearly understood. It is difficult to determine how water will flow in any given geologic formation. In many cases it is simply unknown. Once in the ground, these wastes cannot be removed or controlled in any way. Because the wastes are pumped underground, it is nearly impossible to know where the wastes will eventually end up.

Government regulation of injection wells is minimal, which makes the method attractive to companies charged with disposing of toxic wastes. Other methods of disposal have much more strict regulations, increasing the expense.

▪ *Landfills.* Most solid wastes and household garbage end up in a landfill. Landfills are canyons or large holes that have been dug to dump trash. Often this land is of low value or unsuitable for economic use. Marshes, for example, abandoned mines, gravel pits or limestone sink holes, make good landfills. The problem here is that a landfill is the last place your garbage is moved to after it leaves your home. Garbage is seldom inspected for household or industrial wastes that may be classified as toxic.

Periodically the trash in a landfill is bulldozed and compacted to make room for additional trash. When the hole or canyon is finally filled to capacity, earth is piled on top and then graded. Many former landfills have been used as building sites for residential homes.

Problems arise when buried biodegradable material creates a gas called *methane*, which sometimes leaks through to the atmosphere. Methane is a toxic gas and is flammable, and can harm the atmosphere.

The locations of many older landfills are unknown, which means that residences and public buildings may already be built in contaminated areas.

Ground water contamination by landfill occurs because landfills are often poorly *sited* or located. In other words, the local geology and its nearness to ground water sources have been ignored. Our desire for quick and easy solutions to disposal problems are shortsighted if we don't consider the problems that will be created later by toxic wastes.

The exact number of landfills in the United States is unknown. The best estimates suggest that there are approximately 18,500 municipal landfills, and almost 76,000 industrial sites. The majority of these landfills are not suitable to receive hazardous

Landfills are one of the most common ways that we dispose of garbage in this country. Unfortunately, by burying this waste, landfills inhibit natural processes that could break down much of the waste.

wastes. Unfortunately, due to the widespread use of chemicals in the home and the poor monitoring of these sites, most landfills are suspected of containing some hazardous wastes. Fewer than ten states require regular testing of ground water at these landfills.

- *Surface storage.* The lack of safe landfills and the sheer size of the waste disposal problem has created the need for temporary storage facilities called *impoundments*. These storage areas are holding ponds, pits, or lagoons that store liquid wastes. The wastes are either injected underground, allowed to evaporate, or discharged directly into waterways. The problem, once again, is improper monitoring of the process. In many cases, these impound sites are simply left to leach their toxins into the ground.

The EPA conservatively estimates that there are over 181,000 impound sites across the country. Of these, an incredible 98 percent are within one mile of current or potential drinking water sources. Approximately 70 percent of all industrial impound sites are unlined, which allows unrestricted leaching of toxic wastes into the ground.

As with landfills, most surface sites were chosen because the land was cheap and unsuitable for other commercial use.

▪ *Septic tanks and municipal sewer systems.* Over one-third of all households in America (17 million homes housing 70 million people) use septic tanks for disposal of home waste water. A septic tank breaks down wastes through the use of yeasts and other biological agents. Wastes from toilets, garbage disposals, baths or showers are biodegraded and gradually pumped from the tank through a series of underground channels made of tile or other piping. If used properly, a tank only needs to be emptied by a sewer service or plumber once every five years.

An estimated 800 billion gallons of waste water are discharged from septic tanks each year, representing the largest pollution source in the United States. Because it is delivered directly into the soil, this waste water creates the single largest source of contaminated drinking water in this country.

The EPA estimates that over 40 percent of existing septic tank systems are not working properly. Since one in every four houses being built today will have a septic tank, the problem is expected to grow.

The contamination of ground water by septic tanks can be blamed on two major factors. The first is overcrowding of an area. For example, an urban area containing over 40 homes that use septic systems located within a one-mile radius has been proven to be a prime candidate for ground water contamination. Proper planning can eliminate this problem by restricting high density building or, when unavoidable, creating a municipal sewer treatment plant and system.

The second cause is poor maintenance and improper use of septic systems. Many homeowners attempt to minimize the cost of maintaining their systems by placing septic tank "cleaners" into the system. These cleaners dissolve the sludge that should be pumped out every five years and processed at a sewer treatment facility. The system then ejects both the liquid sludge and the cleaner directly into the soil. This material can contaminate the ground water.

Most septic tank "cleaners" contain *synthetic organic chemicals* (SOCs), which are themselves highly toxic. The EPA reports that septic tank cleaners used in Long Island, New York, alone exceed over 400,000 gallons in one year!

Taking poor care of septic systems, however, is only part of the problem. What goes into the tank other than sludge cleaners and biodegradable material is the real culprit. Americans with septic tank systems dump an incredible array of chemicals—

mostly without thinking—into their garbage disposals and toilets. These materials include pesticides; paint and other coating products; cleaners such as nail polish remover, rug cleaners, laundry soap, etc.; auto products, such as antifreeze, brake fluids, and even motor oil! Unfortunately, a septic tank is designed to break down only biological waste.

It's no wonder that a delicate biological balance within a septic system is impossible to maintain! Many of the SOCs will even combine to make relatively unknown compounds which will literally eat away the tank itself—leading to massive direct contamination of the ground.

Those who depend upon a municipal sewer system to whisk away their waste cause their share of problems, too. The chemical horror that can destroy a balanced septic system does the same thing to city sewers. The cost to the city to correct the problem gets passed on to homeowners.

• *Mining.* Mining operations generate toxic waste in the day-to-day operations of taking metals from the earth. First there is the metal itself. Mine tailings—debris left behind after the ore is extracted and processed—still contain some of the original ore. In the late 1970s, when the price of gold and silver reached a record high, some mine operations reopened just to extract ore from the waste tailings. If left behind, these metals can reach ground water by natural geologic and weathering actions.

With these metals come acids used to leach the metal from the original ores. For example, tungsten, which is used in light bulbs and steel manufacturing, must be leached out of an ore using acid.

Cyanide, a well known poison, is used in the extraction of gold and silver. And these heavy metals are toxic as well.

Acids also occur naturally in mines. When water and oxygen react with a compound called pyrite, they form a mixture of iron and sulfuric acid—a substance that can eat through concrete! Water contaminated with this acid is found mostly in the coal mining regions of the eastern United States. But in all mines, dangerous metals like mercury, arsenic, zinc and nickel are suspended in water.

• *Underground storage tanks.* In the United States today there are between five and seven million underground storage tanks. About 2.5 million of them are underground, and the great majority of these are made of steel. Materials stored in them include home heating oil, industrial petroleum products (gasoline, kerosene, brake fluid), solvents, and hazardous wastes.

The fact that steel is used to make these tanks is important because steel is subject to rust and a rusty tank can leak. The majority of underground tanks are owned by the petroleum industry, and about 15 to 20 percent of them are leaking.

The EPA is at a loss to estimate the total amount of yearly leakage. Estimates range from several hundred thousand to millions of gallons. According to the steel tank industry, an estimated 350,000 tanks will be leaking within five years.

The cost to the petroleum industry in cleanup would be astronomical. To clean up the mess created by only one leaking tank, the city of Provincetown, Massachusetts, spent over $3 million!

• *Agriculture.* The United States has been called the breadbasket of the world for good reason. Approximately 45 percent of the world's food supply is grown in this country. But this great abundance is not produced without cost.

The Midwestern soil, worn and unproductive from the abuses of the late-19th and early-20th centuries, became healthy again only with the help of science. Farmers learned to rotate crops and plan each harvest based on the condition of the soil. They also learned to modify the soil itself with chemicals.

Chief among these chemicals are *nitrates* used in fertilizers. Between 1960 and 1985, the use of commercial fertilizers increased by four times. This resulted in an increase in nitrates in the water runoff that entered the ground water. In 1930 the average use of nitrates was eight pounds per acre. By 1985 this had increased to an average of 283 pounds per acre. The presence of nitrates in water is of great concern, because the human body lacks the ability to convert nitrates to a harmless state. Nitrates are particularly hard on infants.

Farmers also increased the yield of their harvests by controlling unwanted plants, animals, and insects through the use of *pesticides.* These include herbicides, which kill unwanted plants and weeds; insecticides used to kill insect pests; fungicides, designed to kill fungus; and rodenticides, poisons used to kill rodents like rats and mice.

The use of pesticides began during World War II with the widespread use of DDT. Once thought to be harmless, DDT was used by the military to fight diseases like malaria, typhus, cholera, and

Pesticides contain many chemicals that are still not fully researched, so their potential toxicity to livestock and humans is not known. Some pesticides, like DDT, have been banned in the U.S. for years because they have been found to be dangerous.

encephalitis. Today the danger of DDT is well known, and it is no longer being used.

With the creation of SOCs, the petroleum industry produced an explosion of products available to the farmer. Over 40,000 different products using over 1,500 active ingredients account for approximately 1.1 billion pounds of chemically treated products used on fields in the United States each year.

Like the early use of DDT by well-meaning people, today's "chemical soup" found in the nation's waterways is causing increased concern. The fact remains that although some health risks are well known, no one really knows the long-term effects of these toxins.

Animal feedlots where livestock are raised are also a prime source of contamination to the soil. Large numbers of animals confined in a relatively small area create large amounts of animal waste. Acids from urine and nitrates from the solid waste, along with the bacterial elements in both, can migrate to ground water if not managed properly.

Other Pollutants

- *Atmospheric pollution.* Industrial plants frequently emit large quantities of heavy metals and other toxic wastes into the air through inadequate or nonexistent smokestack filters. The most widely known of these pollutants is acid rain, a mixture of sulfur and nitrogen oxides. Acid rain commonly occurs in areas of the country where coal is burned.
- *Transportation of hazardous wastes.* The EPA estimates that 90 percent of the nation's hazardous wastes travel by truck at one time or another. Out of every 11,000 gallons shipped by truck, about 38 gallons is lost in transit. This means about 14 million gallons of toxic material disappear each year, and no one knows what happens to it. There is no way to truly assess the potential harm of these lost materials.
- *Nuclear materials.* No doubt the thought of *radioactive* materials lost in your neighborhood would concern you and your friends. Like an image from a 1950s movie, you might expect any second to see firefighters with protective suits working with

The problem with nuclear waste disposal is so persistent that many facilities are merely temporary storage sites for highly radioactive material until a permanent solution can be found.

radiation counters, only to be attacked by giant ants suddenly appearing from a 20-foot hill in your back yard.

Luckily that stuff only happens in movies. In fact, radioactive materials like metals and biochemicals occur naturally in the process of decay in underground rock beds and geologic formations. If your drinking water flows through these places, it may pick up radioactive particles. High levels of natural radiation, called *radionuclides*, are dependant on geologic location. Uranium, which is naturally radioactive, is found almost exclusively in the west. Specific locations are the Colorado Plateau and Rocky Mountain regions, including some portions of

California, Washington, Texas, and Idaho; and all of Arizona, New Mexico, Oklahoma, Kansas, Montana, Wyoming, and North and South Dakota.

Another source of radioactive material is a gas called *radon*. Radon gas is created due to the decay of uranium in the earth. Radon is odorless, colorless, and can only be detected using special equipment. This gas may enter a home through the basement and cause a health risk. Radon may occur anywhere in the United States, but is most common in the Appalachian region, which extends from Maine down the East Coast to Georgia and Alabama.

Man-made radionuclides are by far the greatest source of radionuclides that exist on earth. Humans have created more than 800 different types of radioactive material through the nuclear industry.

Although the chance of contamination by nuclear materials is slim, some danger remains in two problem areas. First is the mining and refining of uranium, which is used in nuclear power plants. It is estimated that between 530,000 to one million pounds of uranium dust has been emitted into the air from a processing plant in Fernald, Ohio, since the mid 1950s. And this is only one plant!

The second problem area is what to do with nuclear waste. Although highly controlled, as of today the spent fuel rods (that contain the used uranium) and other elements from nuclear power plants amount to 24 million pounds of highly toxic wastes. All of it is currently being stored in temporary sites. By the turn of the century, however, this number is expected to grow to over 100 million pounds, and no

The Three Mile Island nuclear power plant in Harrisburg, Pennsylvania, made history in 1979 when reactor number two (shown by arrow) had to be shut down. The accident released some radioactive steam into the atmosphere, and the reactor became so toxic that it had to be closed permanently.

permanent storage solution has been found.

This material will remain dangerously radioactive for hundreds of thousands of years. Many feel that the potential for disaster is greater than our capability to control this waste.

• *Selenium*. Selenium is another natural source of toxic contamination. In small quantities this mineral is harmless. But when selenium is concentrated, it is absorbed by plant and animal life and can cause illness. For example, fish having high levels of selenium in their bodies have been caught. If these fish are eaten, they can make a person very sick.

Selenium was formed due to ancient volcanic eruptions. Thin layers of selenium have gradually been exposed by the forces of weather and erosion over millions of years. The result is the gradual erosion and concentration of the mineral in marshes and other low-level basins of water.

Then the food chain does its part. Algae, plants, and bacteria are eaten by small fish and animals, who are then eaten in turn by larger predators. In time the mineral consumption accumulates, so that in some areas, eating a freshly caught fish may make you deathly ill.

To date there has been no known cleanup of selenium-contaminated areas.

THREE

DANGERS TO PEOPLE AND OTHER LIVING THINGS

Humans are chemical beings who live in a chemical universe. Without the natural chemicals that make up our bodies, we would cease to exist. Your body maintains a fine chemical balance that can be affected by the ingestion of "foreign" chemicals (chemicals common to your body but ingested at a higher level).

An example is calcium. You may have heard a lot on the news about the ailments of old age that can be helped by increased doses of calcium, commonly found in milk. But too much of this mineral will cause problems with the body's joints, as deposits of calcium can build up and cause great pain.

If you run all day on an athletic field in the heat of the summer, your body loses salt. It needs to be replaced to help stabilize your body during respiration. But too much salt can cause water retention in some people and can lead to blood circulation problems in others.

So when it comes to chemicals, just enough is okay. Too much is bad. Balance is the key.

The problem with most toxic wastes is concentration. Arsenic and cyanide, both common in some foods in trace amounts, are deadly poisons in great amounts. Just like the human body, our ecosystem needs balance. By introducing tons and tons of man-made chemical and nuclear wastes to a relatively balanced natural environment, we create serious health risks.

This freshwater carp is dead, a victim of a polluted river. The object next to the fish is a plastic container that was "non-returnable."

Food manufacturers and water companies do a relatively good job of intercepting these wastes before they contaminate your water and food. However, the problem of toxic elements in our lives can't be eliminated entirely. The following are just a few of the effects of toxic materials on the environment in general, and on you specifically:

- *Air pollution.* Smog interferes with the ability of many plants to convert sunlight to energy. This causes a reduced rate of *photosynthesis*, the name of this process. For example, when a tree is constantly exposed to smog it will stop using its external branches, thereby creating dead leaves and dry branches that can create a fire hazard. The remaining leaves must provide for the entire tree and, failing to do so, may result in the death of the tree.

    Acid rain also kills forests and orchards. In addition, the runoff of acid rain enters lakes and streams, and as these poisons accumulate in the same water bodies, the water becomes poisonous.

- *Nitrates.* Found in fertilizer, nitrates are put into the ground to improve a farm's soil conditions. They are generally not a problem to adults when they are absorbed into the body through the foods we eat. But babies under three months old are vulnerable to blood disorders caused by nitrates.

- *Pesticides.* Exposure to pesticides has been determined to cause many illnesses in humans. Cancer; birth defects; infertility; Parkinson's disease; and other genetic (inherited), reproductive, and central nervous system abnormalities are just a few of the health problems that can occur due to pesticides.

    Logic dictates that if you design a chemical to

California farmworkers' children play in runoff water that probably contains residue from harmful pesticides. This water eventually seeps into the ground, poisoning future sources of drinking water.

kill a specific form of life, it might also harm other forms of life. Most pesticides are untested. The National Academy of Sciences reports that only 10 of 3,350 ingredients used in pesticides have complete data available about their effect on human health.

The tradeoff in using pesticides for farming can be summarized this way: Do we want to continue feeding much of the world's population, or do we want to reduce the damage to the environment at the cost of greatly reducing our crop yield? Many farmers are now working with organic (natural) methods of fertilization and pest control to see if they can produce as much food at comparable costs and in similar quantities. But no easy answers are in sight.

▪ *Nuclear wastes.* Like chemicals, the harm that nuclear radiation can cause is dependant upon the rate of exposure over a period of time. Radiation can kill or damage cells. If enough of the cells die within a specific body organ, that organ will die. Eventually, too much radiation leads to death.

Low radiation is also a problem. If low doses of radiation kill a few cells but not the organism, these cells can be replaced. But if the cell is only damaged, it can continue to duplicate its damaged form. Damage to an ordinary cell—like bone or organ tissue—may result in cancer. Damage to a reproductive cell can cause genetic damage, leading to birth defects. Low doses given for chest X-rays and dental work, however, have been proven to be quite harmless.

Other serious effects of radiation exposure are birth defects and cancer in infants. The fetus (an unborn baby) is very vulnerable to radiation damage. The known effects of radiation on the fetus include abnormal skeletal and central nervous system development. Genetic effects, including changes in the body's DNA (the cell's "key" to reproducing itself), can cause hereditary problems and disease.

- *Chemical and mineral "soup."* There is no known way to determine the effects of toxins on life with the infinite possible combinations that exist in toxic waste sites. Simply put, no one knows. To merely list the known effects of the few chemicals where data exists would require more space than we have here. It is sufficient to say that most scientists agree cancer is at the top of the list. There are hundreds of different cancers: some rare, some common.

No one knows for sure what causes many forms of cancer, but we do know how devastating its effects can be. When toxic wastes play a role in making people sick, the results are even more disturbing. One tragic example of this occurred not too long ago in a neighborhood near Niagara Falls, New York, called Love Canal.

Love Canal

An increase in cancer and other diseases became obvious to the residents of Love Canal in the 1960s. In time they learned that they and their children were victims of a chemical soup that had been stored in an abandoned canal. After much investigation, the story emerged.

A canal built by William T. Love in the 1890s for generating electricity had been sold to the

Love Canal first brought the problem of toxic waste to the attention of Americans after families were forced to leave their homes. Fumes and chemicals in the ground around their homes made people ill.

Niagara Power and Development Company. They gave permission to the Hooker Electrochemical Company to use the site as a chemical waste dump. Between 1942 and 1952, over 21,000 tons of various chemicals wastes were dumped at the site. In 1953 the site was covered over with earth.

No one could guess that years later the wastes buried there would impact over 500 homes and cost the government more than $22 million. And nothing was cleaned up. The money went for purchasing the neighborhood and the many lawsuits that followed. This former residential site was boarded up and abandoned, complete with warning signs. The cost to human life is still undetermined.

The Love Canal incident is significant because as a result of this tragedy, many new laws regarding toxic waste were passed. Concerned citizens became deeply suspicious of the corporations and government officials who tried to cover up harmful details about toxic waste. If it had not been for Love Canal, much legislation intended to protect our health and "clean-up funds" such as Superfund would not exist today.

Times Beach

Times Beach, Missouri, holds the sad distinction of being the only town in the United States purchased by the U.S. government. The price was more than $33 million, and the reason was toxic waste. Over 2,200 residents had to be relocated.

The problem in Times Beach began when contaminated oil was sprayed on the town roads to control dust. Discovered too late, the oil had been

Radiation Hazards

Every living thing on this planet is constantly exposed to radiation from natural sources in the earth and from cosmic rays that strike the earth.

This whole-body exposure rate is well within safe ranges. The following is a breakdown of what types of radiation the average person receives annually:

Natural sources (earth and cosmic)	85.00 millirems
Medical sources (X-rays)	70.00 millirems
Fallout	3.00 millirems
Miscellaneous (Unknown)	2.00 millirems
On the job	.80 millirems
Nuclear power	.01 millirems
TOTAL	**160.81 millirems**

The millirem measures the amount of radiation absorbed by any material, such as human tissue. A millirem is one 1,000th of a rem.

How much exposure to radiation is harmful? Exposure to just 400 rems during a brief period can be lethal.

mixed with a type of chemical called *dioxin*. Dioxin has been proven to cause cancer and is considered to be highly toxic.

Once again, a noticeable increase in illness in the town prompted an investigation. The dioxin-contaminated soils were exposing residents to over 1,100 times the amount the EPA considers safe for dioxins.

Today, the entire town, like the neighborhood at Love Canal, is abandoned. Danger signs warn passers by to stay away. ◆

FOUR

GETTING RID OF THE PROBLEM

With millions of tons of toxic wastes being generated each year, the problem of safe disposal of these wastes has become a major national issue. Unfortunately, to date there are only a few options open. Each method of disposal has become controversial and questions of safety persist.

As explained earlier, approximately 60 percent of the toxic waste disposed of legally is placed in injection wells for permanent storage. The goal is to trap the wastes between layers of impermeable rock (rock that fluid cannot penetrate), thereby preventing their spread to ground water. The well itself is fed through a steel pipe surrounded in concrete to prevent leakage. When a given site is determined to be *saturated* (full), the well is capped and sealed permanently.

The flaw in this method is that often there is no limit to the directions the underground waste may travel. Pumping fluid waste under pressure can force the waste to find weaknesses in the rock and flow in undesirable directions. The waste does what it does naturally: It is following the path of least resistance. The result is that, despite the effort to locate geological "traps" for liquid wastes, no one can be totally sure of any site. If the waste finds cracks in the containing layers of rock, it may find its way into some source of ground water and perhaps up to the surface.

In 1984, a series of wells in Ohio run by Chemical Waste Management Company leaked an estimated 45 million gallons of acid and other

Onondaga Lake in Syracuse, New York, is one of the most polluted lakes in the United States, due to heavy industrial waste dumping. But cyclists may still use the bike trail that rings the lake.

wastes into an adjacent sandstone site. Sandstone is very *porous*, like a sponge, so that fluid travels through it easily. The company was fined $10 million by the state of Ohio. The cause of the leak was determined to be cracks in the wells caused by corrosion.

Toxic Burial

The Chemical Waste Management Company also runs the nation's largest landfill for toxic wastes —a chalk pit covering 2,400 acres in Emille, Alabama. Company officials believe that the 700-foot thickness of the chalk layer surrounding the site will keep the wastes safely stored for 10,000 years.

Wastes are deposited in the pit like a giant, multi-layered cake. As trucks unload the toxic waste containers, giant bulldozers crush and compact the waste and the barrels in which they were shipped. When a given layer is leveled out, they cover it with chalk and cement dust to neutralize the acids. When it is full to capacity, this site will be capped with clay and surrounded with special wells. Monitors will check the conditions underground for leakage.

Although this site is believed to be the nation's safest toxic waste landfill, the EPA feels that all land-fills will eventually leak. It has therefore forbidden the burial of high-hazard liquids.

One of the safest places in which toxic waste has been stored is an abandoned salt mine in Heringen, Germany. More than 2,300 feet below ground, the mine is geologically stable, dry, and deep enough to prohibit accidental access. The tox-ins are kept in their original storage barrels to ease monitoring. To date, over two million barrels of toxic wastes have been stored here.

Chevron's El Segundo, California, facility has begun using a clever new method of removing oil spilled on the ground. Bacteria that occurs naturally in soil is used to actually consume the oil, because the bacteria thrive on hydrocarbons found in it. They convert the oil into harmless carbon dioxide and water. These bacteria were one method used in the 1991 Persian Gulf War to help clean up the world's largest oil spill.

Michigan State University is also experiment-ing with bacteria used to remove chlorine atoms from toxic wastes. This method makes waste less

How Large Is The Radioactive Waste Problem?

To date the total radioactive waste generated in this country includes the following:

• Roughly 306,000 cubic meters of high-level wastes (mostly liquid) from defense programs, nearly all of which are located at government facilities;

• 4,626 cubic meters of highly radioactive spent (used) fuel rods from nuclear reactors, most of which are stored at nuclear power plants;

• 3,080,000 cubic meters of low-level radioactive wastes (contaminated work gloves, tools, medical isotopes, irradiated reactor components, etc.);

• 96,500,000 cubic meters of radioactive tailings from active uranium mining and processing, almost all mines being located in sparsely populated regions of Arizona, New Mexico, Utah, and Wyoming.

dangerous so that other, less-hardy bacteria can convert the remaining waste matter.

A process called *vitrification* is being developed by Battelle Pacific Northwest Laboratories of Richland, Washington. This process fuses contaminated soil into a glasslike substance that is more durable than marble or granite. Electrodes are placed in the soil to convert the soil into a molten mass as hot as 3,000 degrees Fahrenheit. As the soil cools, it solidifies. In some cases, contaminated areas may be rendered harmless in place, without costly (and dangerous) removal.

Solvent recycling is the sole business of the Oil and Solvent Process Company of Azusa, California, which processes about six million gallons of solvent each year. That's a lot of solvent that can be used again instead of adding to the disposal problem.

Ocean Dumping

Finally, a process known as *ocean incineration* is widely used to destroy and discard toxic wastes. Ships at sea equipped with specially designed incineration furnaces process wastes at 1800 degrees Fahrenheit. Fish are then placed in special tanks treated with the processed waste to determine the effectiveness of the process. If the fish live 24 hours, the processed waste is considered safe enough to be dumped into the ocean.

In Europe the ocean incineration process has been used continually, but in the United States the process was halted temporarily for several reasons. First, the process guarantees a maximum rate of destruction of 99 percent—sometimes less. Although the remaining one percent may seem insignificant, over time it adds up to millions of tons of waste that can still do damage to the environment.

Another problem is that ocean incineration only works on about 20 percent of the most common toxic wastes. Given that a lot of variable mixing of wastes from different sources occurs, some of the toxins present will not be destroyed. Some ecological damage can't be avoided.

The findings of the EPA indicate that as much as 10 to 20 percent of the hazardous wastes generated in the United States each year could be incinerated. That's 250 million metric tons. Nearly half of these wastes are liquids that could be incinerated at sea. The demand for these services is likely to increase over time. But despite the expected demand, the industry itself is still operating far below the rate that is needed to burn these wastes.

A Continuing Effort

Although options for disposal of wastes are currently being developed, it is unlikely that these technologies can be ready in time to meet the demand. In other words, the sheer number of wastes that need to be disposed of exceeds the capability of any solutions.

Despite illegal dumping and the occasional criminal mislabeling of toxins, American industry is sensitive to the toxic waste problem and is cooperating with government and other groups in trying to solve it. In a real sense, this problem snuck up on us. When toxic wastes were first produced, little thought was given to the danger of disposal.

This volunteer is examining the debris on a Lake Michigan beach. Trash dumped on beaches and offshore is a major problem. Dangerous items, including old hypodermic needles, have been found.

There are no easy answers. Today we inject toxic wastes underground and bury them in land-fills. We store them on the surface in barrels, ponds, and warehouses. We turn them into glass and we burn them prior to dumping them into the sea. There are also government programs, industry research projects, and small businesses with innovative ideas reaching for solutions. But none of these plans or solutions will be enough.

The problem is the age-old battle between money and the environment. Those who generate these wastes make cleanup decisions based on cost. Many environmentalists say that what is needed is learning one simple fact: Cleaning up the mess costs more than properly handling the problem in the first place.

FIVE

WHAT'S BEING DONE?

Now that you have some idea of the magnitude of the toxic waste problem, it might seem like the outlook for the future is bleak. But like all mistakes humans make—even huge ones such as toxic waste—we can benefit from experience and, hopefully, improve our future.

Remember, toxins are only one small part of the pollution problem. It is recognized now as being a major problem because of the heightened environmental awareness that began to emerge in the 1960s. In recent years citizen action groups have brought environmental concerns to the attention of our leaders. Today the government has begun to respond by looking for ways to cure old problems and prevent new ones.

After World War II, the United States enjoyed industrial growth on a scale unlike any time in history. There was the introduction of new "miracle" products: plastics, synthetic fabrics, coated paper goods, bleaches, cleaners, and electronic goods.

Waste management—the organized disposal of waste—became an issue as, quite literally, the garbage began to pile up. In 1965 Congress passed the Solid Waste Disposal Act, the first federal law to require safeguards and encourage environmentally sound methods for the disposal of all wastes.

On April 22, 1970, the first Earth Day was celebrated in the United States. Now we celebrate Earth Week each year. The year of the first Earth Day also saw passage of the Environmental Education Act. In

This truck will take toxic industrial wastes from a factory site to a "safe" place of disposal. Today, all U.S. manufacturers must take precautions to dispose of toxins safely. In the future, perhaps industry will use and produce fewer dangerous materials.

1970 Congress passed the Resource Recovery Act, and in 1976 passed the Resource Conservation and Recovery Act (RCRA). Since then, the RCRA has been amended continuously as our knowledge of the handling of wastes grows.

The RCRA has the following specific goals:
- To protect human health and the environment from the potential hazards of waste disposal;
- To conserve energy and natural resources;
- To reduce the amount of waste generated, including hazardous wastes;

- To ensure that wastes are managed in an environmentally sound manner.

The goals were amended by Congress in 1984 to increase the scope of RCRA and begin dealing with specifically hazardous wastes. Called the Hazardous and Solid Waste Amendments (HSWA), these changes expanded RCRA to deal with the direct control and reduction of toxic wastes.

These HSWA were a direct result of citizens voicing concern over existing methods of hazardous waste disposal. Landfills, in particular, were not safe.

A companion law to RCRA and its amendments was passed in 1980 to clean up past mistakes such as inactive or abandoned hazardous wastes sites. This law is called the Comprehensive Environmental Response, Compensation and Liability Act, or CERCLA. It has a more popular name: Superfund.

Understanding how these laws work together can be quite confusing. Often the term "RCRA" is used to mean several different things: the law itself, its specific regulations, and EPA policy in general. Actually the law describes the waste management program ordered by Congress and gives EPA the authority or power to develop it.

Enforcement

The regulations portion of RCRA carries out the intent of Congress and provides explicit requirements for waste management that are legally enforceable. This part of RCRA literally tells the waste generators, users, transporters, and disposers of toxic waste how to do their job, thereby protecting the public from possible accidents. "Legally enforce-

This worker is removing lead particles from rooftops in a Texas neighborhood near a manufacturing site. In other areas in the U.S., many homes and businesses have had to replace building insulation using asbestos, a highly toxic material.

able" means that if you break a regulation of RCRA, you can be arrested. If convicted you have to go to jail, pay a fine and, if a spill occurred, pay for the cleanup of the spill.

The EPA guidance documents and policy directives help make clear to both the public and to enforcement people just how the regulations apply to a given situation.

Although this is a good start, RCRA does not completely cover the toxic waste problem. Specifically stated in the law are some critical areas that are not covered, including the following:

- *Domestic sewage.*

- *Irrigation waters or industrial discharges* permitted under the Federal Water Pollution Control Act. Here is a case where multiple laws intending to remedy the same problem may be in conflict. By ignoring such a mistake, the problem often continues despite the laws designed to stop it.

- Certain *nuclear material* (as defined by the Atomic Energy Act). The Department of Energy regulates the use of all nuclear materials in this country.

- Certain *mining wastes*, such as uranium.

- *Agricultural wastes*, excluding some pesticides. This, some critics believe, is the result of powerful lobbies that protect the interests of the agriculture industry. These lobbies object to the high cost of pesticide regulation.

- Small *quantity wastes,* that is, wastes from businesses generating fewer than 220 pounds of hazardous waste per month. Is 220 pounds per month too little to be bothersome? Not necessarily. Consider this: At that rate, a small business can discard about

Old appliances often contain *freon*, a gas that has been found to harm the earth's ozone layer.

2,640 pounds of toxic materials each year. That's roughly 1.25 tons per business. Imagine for a moment 16,000 businesses in an area the size of Los Angeles. If each business discards only 220 pounds of toxic waste each month, everything is legal. But that's still a lot of dumping. Remember that Love Canal had 21,000 tons dumped in it over a period of ten years. Fortunately, there are state and local laws that often regulate minor dumping.

Superfund

Superfund—the group of laws dealing with the cleanup of abandoned toxic sites—is not without its problems. The first is money. The EPA estimates

Environmental Laws

The following is a list of laws that regulate hazardous substances. The agency responsible for enforcing the law is listed in parentheses.

ATOMIC ENERGY ACT (Nuclear Regulatory Commission). Regulates nuclear energy production and nuclear waste disposal.

CLEAN AIR ACT (EPA). Regulates the emission of hazardous air pollutants.

CLEAN WATER ACT (EPA). Regulates the discharge of hazardous pollutants into the nation's surface waters.

COMPREHENSIVE ENVIRONMENTAL RESPONSE, COMPENSATION, AND LIABILITY ACT (Superfund/EPA). Provides for the cleanup of inactive and abandoned hazardous waste sites.

HAZARDOUS MATERIALS TRANSPORTATION ACT (U.S. Dept. of Transportation). Regulates the transportation of hazardous materials.

MARINE PROTECTION, RESEARCH, AND SANCTUARIES ACT (EPA). Regulates waste disposal offshore.

OCCUPATIONAL SAFETY AND HEALTH ACT, U.S. Occupational Safety and Health Administration (OSHA). Regulates hazards in the workplace, including worker exposure to hazardous wastes.

RESOURCE CONSERVATION AND RECOVERY ACT (EPA). Regulates hazardous waste generation, storage, transportation, treatment, and disposal.

SAFE DRINKING WATER ACT (EPA). Regulates contaminant levels in drinking water.

SURFACE MINING CONTROL AND RECLAMATION ACT (U.S. Dept. of the Interior). Regulates the environmental aspects of mining (particularly coal) and soil reclamation.

TOXIC SUBSTANCES CONTROL ACT (EPA). Regulates the manufacture, use, and disposal of chemical substances.

that the cost of cleaning up just one minor site, such as a small industrial site, may be close to $6 million. A major site can cost up to ten times this amount. Considering the fact that there are thousands of abandoned toxic dumps in this country, potential cleanup costs will run into the billions of dollars.

The second problem is liability. Under RCRA laws, the EPA is charged with recovering the cost of the cleanup of Superfund sites. The problem here lies in tangled legal webs that often make it impossible to reach the original source of the waste. There is no way to estimate the legal costs that may occur as a result of action against those responsible.

But there are definite benefits to these laws. Businesses trying to save money helped create the toxic waste problem in the first place. To save dollars today, businesses must learn that poorly managed waste is their most costly problem. Not only does the wise business executive consider the cost of disposal, but he or she looks for ways to minimize waste to begin with. This saves not only natural resources, but the costly disposal process as well.

Under RCRA, the EPA is charged with the monitoring, regulation, and enforcement of toxics from the *point of generation*—such as a factory—to the users, transporters, and ultimate disposal or destruction. Chief among the EPA's strategy to reduce its own workload and the risk to the environment is the encouragement of waste reduction. The following are EPA's specific approaches to waste reduction:

- *Source separation* (or segregation). This keeps hazardous wastes from contaminating wastes that are not hazardous. This method requires that businesses

Aerosol cans used to contain *chlorofluorohydrocarbons*, or CFCs for short, until the U.S. government banned their use. CFCs were found to damage the ozone content of our atmosphere, and ozone is essential to life on earth because it deflects harmful cosmic radiation from the sun.

(and others) establish a practice of being careful to keep these types of waste separate. This is the cheapest way to reduce the huge volume of hazardous wastes.

- *Recycling.* Many industries now recycle chemicals to reduce costs of use and disposal. Solvents and oil products are the leaders in this field.
- *Substitution of raw material.* This process encourages industry to switch from raw materials that are highly toxic to those that are not but still accomplish the same thing.
- *Manufacturing process changes.* This means encouraging a change in how things are made to reduce or eliminate the production of hazardous wastes.
- *Substitution of products.* The EPA encourages industry to use products that not only limit toxins when manufactured, but do not produce any toxic material at all.

WHAT CAN YOU DO?

Remember
that the law as it
exists in the prac-
tical world is in
itself an ever- changing thing. We may hear about rich industry tycoons fighting to keep things as they are. We may become disappointed at how slowly things are moving. But the environment has become a genuine concern to many industries, and this awareness has resulted in a surprising number of business leaders who are changing their way of doing business. The problems of our past are still with us, however, and we all need to examine what we as individuals can do to help.

You and your friends can do a great deal of good in helping reduce toxic waste the same way that government and industry does.

The first place you can start is with the toxins in your own home. In effect, you can become a mini-EPA by following these simple steps:

- *Read labels.* Learn the kinds of products you buy and use around the house that may be hazardous. For example, the batteries in your portable radio may not seem like much, but multiplied by the millions that get thrown away each day, and eventually the toxins in these batteries will leak into the environment. If the EPA won't let an auto shop improperly throw away a car battery, what makes your little batteries different? Flashlight batteries don't have liquid acid, but they do have a heavy metal called lead. And this is just one example. Your house is full of toxic materials, from oven cleaners to nail polish.

- *Only discard empty containers.* You might think

Many of the products you use in your home and garden are toxic, and by using or disposing of them improperly, you make the problem of toxic waste even worse. Learn what you can do to help the environment.

Recycling metal, like old automobiles, is an important way that we can conserve natural resources and prevent harmful waste from ruining our environment. Smaller items, like plastic water jugs, glass bottles, and newspapers, should also be recycled to save energy, resources and landfills.

that a little bit of bleach or solvent or cleaner left in the container can't do much. But if thousands of people throw away small amounts of these substances, those little amounts quickly become tons.

- *Learn how to store wastes.* Contact the local fire department and find out where the local household hazardous waste facility is. Learn what you can mix with what. Mixing chemicals together is very dangerous. Some may produce a fatal gas, or catch fire spontaneously.
- *Select the least hazardous products* for your own use. For example, a water-based paint is less toxic than an oil-based paint.
- *Buy multi-purpose cleaners.* When selecting a cleaner, pick one that does more than one job.
- *Follow directions carefully.* Use as little as possible. Twice as much is not always twice as good—it's wasteful and expensive as well.
- *Get involved.* Let your parents or other adults know if you see someone dumping any kind of trash improperly. It may not be toxic, but you don't know for sure. Solid, non-toxic wastes also have proper disposal places. People you see doing illegal "dumping" probably know what they're doing. Do not challenge them directly, but tell someone who can make them stop, such as your own local disposal company.

Many illegal dumpers have been brought to justice and the damage to the environment reduced because of citizen actions. The EPA encourages people to report knowledge of illegal dumping.

The RCRA goes even further in promoting citizen action by including the following statutes in the law:

Any battery—for flashlights or cars—contains unsafe materials that do not disappear even when the battery has lost its usefulness. Unfortunately, Americans dispose of batteries and other dangerous materials without thinking of the problems they can create.

- Citizens have, by law, access to information obtained by the EPA or the states about a facility under investigation for illegal toxic waste disposal.
- Citizens are allowed to participate in the permit or licensing process of new industrial facilities if they will be sources of toxic waste.
- Citizens may bring lawsuits against anyone whose hazardous waste management may cause endangerment.

- Citizens may bring a lawsuit against anyone who may be violating a RCRA permit, standard, or requirement.
- The EPA or the state must notify local officials, and post a sign at sites that pose an imminent and substantial threat to human health and the environment. If you know of such a place in your community, you have the right to be informed of what is being done to protect the environment and the community.

For More Information

If you want to learn more about toxic waste and disposal, you may write to the following:

U.S. Environmental Protection Agency
401 M Street, S.W.
Washington, D.C. 20460

GLOSSARY

ACID RAIN. Pollutants in the atmosphere that fall to earth with rain, slowly poisoning waterways and plant life.

BIODEGRADABLE. Substances that can be broken down into simple, organic parts and returned to the environment naturally.

DIOXIN. A toxic chemical known to cause cancer. Dioxin was found in unsafe levels throughout the town of Times Beach, Missouri.
DDT. A pesticide banned by the U.S. government because it was found to be too toxic to humans.

ENVIRONMENTAL PROTECTION AGENCY (EPA). The federal agency charged with safeguarding the environment.

IMPOUNDMENT. A temporary storage area for toxic waste.
INJECTION WELL. A site where wastes are pumped into an underground well.

LANDFILL. A site where garbage or toxic wastes are buried.

NITRATES. A variety of salts, some of which are used in fertilizer.

OCEAN INCINERATION. Burning wastes at sea and then dumping them into the ocean.

PARTICULATES. Particles found in the atmosphere.

PESTICIDES. A family of chemical compounds used to kill unwanted plants, insects, fungi and other pests that can harm crops.

PHOTOSYNTHESIS. The process that plants use to convert sunlight into energy for growth. Smog and acid rain can interfere with photosynthesis.

RADIOACTIVE WASTE. Waste that gives off energy in the form of particles or rays that are harmful to life.

RADON. A odorless, colorless gas that is produced by the decay of uranium in the earth. Radon has been found in homes, posing a health risk.

SEPTIC TANK. A disposal system for household wastes and waste water.

SUPERFUND. The nickname given to the U.S. Comprehensive Environmental Response, Compensation, and Liability Act. The "super fund" is money used to clean up toxic waste sites.

SYNTHETIC ORGANIC CHEMICALS (SOCs). Laboratory-produced substances that are used as substitutes for organic chemicals (chemicals occurring naturally in nature). Many SOCs are used in agriculture.

TOXIC WASTE. Waste that is harmful to life.

TOXINS. Any substance that is *toxic*, or harmful to life.

VITRIFICATION. A process that fuses contaminated soils into a hard substance to render it harmless.

Bibliography

Books

Brezina, Dennis W. and Allen Overmyer. *Congress In Action*. New York: The Free Press/Macmillan Publishing, 1974.

Davis, Lee Niedringhaus. *The Corporate Alchemists*. New York: William Morrow,1984.

Facing America's Trash. Congress of the United States, Office of Technology Assessment (OTA-O-424), 1989.

Levine, Adeline G. *Love Canal*. Lexington, MA: Lexington Books/D. C. Heath, 1982.

Long, Robert E., ed. *The Problem of Waste Disposal*. New York: H. W. Wilson Co., 1989.

The Nuclear Waste Primer. New York: League of Women Voters/Nick Lyons Books,1985.

Ocean Dumping of Waste Material. Hearings from the Subcommittee on Fisheries and Wildlife Conservation, Congress of the United States. U.S. Govt. Printing Office, Washington D.C., 1988.

Ocean Incineration. Congress of the United States, Office of Technology Assessment (OTA-O-313), 1986.

Rosenbaum, Walter A. *Environmental Politics and Policy*. Washington, D.C.: Congressional Quarterly, 1990.

Shapo, Marshall S. *A Nation of Guinea Pigs*. New York: The Free Press/Macmillan Publishing, 1979.

Stewart, John Cary. *Drinking Water Hazards*. Hiram, Ohio: Envirographics, 1990.

Whelan, Dr. Elizabeth. *Toxic Terror*. Ottawa, Illinois: Jameson Books, 1985.

Periodicals

Blackwell, Marjorie. "Buried Toxics." *Northern California Real Estate Journal*, December, 1986.

Boraiko, Allen A. "Storing Up Trouble...Hazardous Waste." *National Geographic*, March 1985.

Harris, Tom. "Selenium: The Poisoning of America." *Sacramento Bee*, December 5, 1988.

Kazak, Don. "No Simple Solutions." *Palo Alto Weekly*, January 18, 1989.

Meadows, Donnella H. "When 'Cleanup' of Hazardous Messes is a Misnomer." *Los Angeles Times*, April 16, 1989.

Parrish, Michael. Warning: Danger Below. *Los Angeles Times*, November 6, 1989.

Schrage, Michael. "A 'Steve Jobs' of Garbage Could Clean Up." *Los Angeles Times*, January 11, 1990.

Pamphlets

A Home Buyer's Guide to Environmental Hazards. U.S. Environmental Protection Agency (CA114U08/90), 1990.

Solving the Hazardous Waste Problem. U.S. Environmental Protection Agency (EPA/530-SW-86-037), 1986.

Toxic Chemicals In My Home? County of Los Angeles, May 1986.

Toxics Around Us. KRON-TV, San Francisco, 1990.

Waste Minimization. U.S. Environmental Protection Agency (EPA/530-SW-026), 1987.

Index

Photo Credits